On the Moon

With thanks to Stuart Atkinson for information about the Moon missions
Managing Editor: Gillian Doherty
Photographs © NASA; photographs of Earth © Digital Vision

On the Moon

Anna Milbourne

Illustrated by Benji Davies

Designed by Laura Fearn

The Moon is very,
very far away.

What do you think it
would be like to go there?

A few people have been to the Moon.
Astronauts went there to see what it was like.

If you went to the Moon
you'd be an astronaut too.

To get to the Moon, you have to go in a huge rocket.

Five...

four...

three...

two...

one...

Lift off!

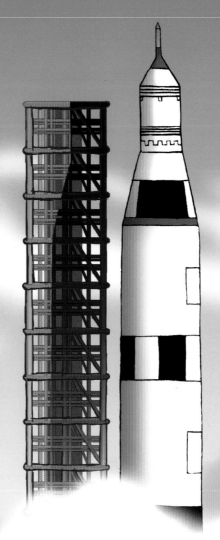

The astronauts sit in a tiny cabin at the very top.

The rocket flies into space.

There's nothing but stars and darkness all around.

It takes four whole days to reach the Moon.

When you get there,
you climb into a
little spaceship.

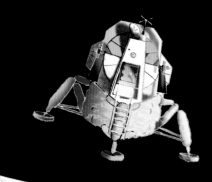

It flies down...

and down...

and lands gently on the Moon.

To go outside, you have to put on a space suit.

There is no air on the Moon.
Space suits carry air so you can breathe.

The Moon is silent, empty and dusty.

When you walk around,
you take big, bouncing strides.

You can jump really far –
much further than you can at home.

Astronauts sometimes go exploring in Moon buggies.

Astronauts put a flag on the Moon to show they have been there.

You can see our world from the Moon.

It looks tiny because it is so far away.

When it's time to go, the astronauts blast off for home.

Do you think you'll ever go to the Moon?